A Cornish Hotchpotch

by

Kathleen Hawke

TRURAN

**First published in 1989
by Dyllansow Truran
Trewolsta, Trewirgie, Redruth, Kernow (Cornwall)**

Copyright © Kathleen Hawke

ISBN 1 85022 048 4

CONTENTS

TIME BRINGS CHANGES

Time brings changes and we must move with the times, or so we are told. Be that as it may, it is pleasant sometimes to wander down memory's lane and recall the halcyon days of the early 1900s when summers always seemed to have been fine and snow seemed non-existent.

Folks led more leisurely lives and more or less followed a daily routine. Country folk went to town on market day to do their business and meet their friends and relatives. Sometimes it became necessary for a policeman to interfere and break up a conversation if it went on too long and obstructed the traffic.

Horses and traps were used by the farming community for conveying their produce and the farmer's wife would sit in the old market house to sell her butter and eggs. It must have been a chilly place in winter. One farmer once confided to another that he had put his clean shirt on over his working one because it was too cold to change but he didn't want his 'missus' to know. A farmer's wife who had been picking fruit to take to market sent her niece to tell her husband, who was working elsewhere, that she was going in to strep (strip), meaning change her clothes.

Folk who had no transport of their own either walked to town or went by the horse-drawn 'bus. It was said that there was always room for one more in the St. Just 'bus which took an hour to go to Penzance and ninety minutes on the return journey. It carried sixteen passengers but would take thirty at a squeeze and younger passengers often walked up the hills to relieve the weight for the horses.

WASHDAY

What a shock Granny would get! In her day Monday was washday, come what may except, perhaps, Feast Monday. Very often if there was something special taking place, the lady of the house "rose" to wash, which meant getting up at 5am – and what a performance it was!

The long tray, with a soap holder each end, came out of its hiding place with the wooden boxes on which it stood; there was also a galvanized bath for the "blueing" water. If one boiled the "whites" the fire would have been lit previously, but when a boiler was used this was done on the "slab" (cooking range) and then the old punching stick went into action. This was part of a shovel "hilt" (handle) cut down to size and scrubbed lily-white.

Water was fetched either from a rain water tank, or pumped or drawn from a well. A galvanized washing board considerably eased the task of cleaning badly soiled garments. After all the clothes had been washed, the first water was replaced by the streaming water and unless there were two at work the water had to be dipped out.

A square of Reckitt's blue was placed in the blue bag for "blueing" and Colman's starch, prepared in a bowl, was used to stiffen summer dresses, pinafores, tablecloths, bedroom and fireplace drapes and vallances. Men's collars and fronts were stiffly starched, as were serviettes used for visitors. On one occasion the farm lad washed his hands in a bowl of starch remarking that it was some funny water! It was not unusual to see clothes spread on hedges to dry.

A WASHDAY RHYME

They that wash on Monday, have all the week to dry,
They that wash on Tuesday, are not so much awry,
They that wash on Wednesday, are not so much to blame,
They that wash on Thursday, wash for shame,
They that wash on Friday, wash in need,
But they that wash on Saturday, are sluts indeed.

THE SLAB OR APPARATUS

The "slab", or "apparatus", were names by which the old black cooking range was known, some of which were gems to use and others which would try the patience of a saint. This was probably due to the position of one's dwelling. In windy weather if one lived on a hill-top, the stove would most likely go like the blazes with the cook "sweating drops" quenching its appetite. A stove in a house in a dip would sometimes need the back door open according to which way the wind was blowing , or maybe one would have to keep it shut and open a window. And what a job it was keeping it clean – what with brushing the flues with soot flying everywhere, and blacklead too. Zebo, a liquid polish, wasn't much better, but the final result was pleasing, with shining brass and steelwork completing the burnishing-leaving the worker as black as a tinker.

DEAR AS SAFFRON

"Dear as saffron" was an old saying widely used, but, although it still applies as saffron has reached a colossal price, not so much of it is used today. Friday was usually baking day and Saturday was spent cleaning up for Sunday.

Saffron cake or buns were the mainstay for "croust" or "crib", according to the area in which one lived (for the uninitiated – mid-morning break). On special occasions, such as Christmas or the parish feast, extra goodness (fat) was used. A relative was a wizard with yeast. Some folks had difficulty in getting their yeast cake to plum (rise) but her's used to "plum up 'ansum" and if she wasn't quite ready to bake it she would clench her fist and push it down again. Prior to 1923 she did her baking in a cloam oven which is still in situ in the old farmhouse in which she lived. She always maintained that food tasted better cooked that way.

In his book "Cornish Homes and Customs", A.K. Hamilton Jenkin tell us that in the early days of immigration to the Rand, the curiosity of the postal authorities was aroused by the number of strange smelling packets passing through their hands. At length an order was given that one of these should be opened. On inspection its contents were adjudged to be a rank poison and the package was accordingly returned to the sender with a stern warning pointing out the nature of the offence. The packets, of course, contained saffron sent from Cornwall to relatives abroad.

Fore Street   St. Austell

THEY USED TO BE ½d PER DOZEN

According to Rhona Churchill (from an odd newspaper cutting) eggs cost a halfpenny a dozen in the 14th century, spiralling to the dizzy price of 3d per dozen in the days of Good Queen Bess.

The West Briton of November 30th, 1821 stated that the price of provisions in the Penzance market was perhaps lower than in any other part of the country. Pork was sold there, by the quarter, for 2d per lb. The price of beef was from 2d to 3d per lb, mutton from 3d to 4d and potatoes fetched 2d for 10 lbs. It should be noted that these were market prices – "Saturday night prices would have been much lower".

Snippets from farm diaries –

1877 –   Eggs 8d per dozen; Butter 1s-6d per pound
1892 –   Eggs 9d per dozen; Butter 1s-5½d per pound
           Pork 4¾d per pound (dead weight)

           120 pilchards 6d
           100 herrings 7½d
           33 mackerel 1s

Prices 1950 –

           3 lbs plain flour 9d
           3 lbs self-raising flour 1s-0½
           Granulated sugar 5d per ½ pound
           Butter 2s per pound
           Margarine 5d per ½ pound
           Cheese 1s-2d per pound
           Sultanas 1s per pound
           ½ lb tea 11d
           Vinegar 6½d per pint
           Tomatoes 9d per pound
           Coal 5s-1½d per cwt.
           Anthracite 6s-3½d per cwt.

The following is a list of provisions supplied by Waters Bros. Newlyn, for the Silver Jubilee Fete at Sancreed on May 6th, 1935 –

40 lbs Saffron cake at 8d per lb	£1. 6.8
20 lbs Sultana cake at 8d per lb	13.4
22 lbs Slab cake at 8d per lb	14.8
50 lbs Genoa cake at 8d per lb	£1.13.4
22 lbs Almond cake at 8d per lb	14.8
26 lbs Madeira cake at 8d per lb	17.4
22 lbs Seed cake at 8d per lb	14.8
11 doz. ¾lb Buns at 6/- per doz.	£3. 6.0
3 x 4 White loaves at 8d	2.0
4 x 4 Brown loaves at 4d	1.4
100 doz. Splits at 4d	£1.13.4
8 lbs Tea at 2/- per lb	16.0
12 lbs Lump Sugar at 3d per lb	3.0

£12.16.4

First & Last House, Lands End.

5

IN A CORNISH KITCHEN

Composer unknown

Why blee'ee, you knows all about it,
'Afore I do tell 'ee a word,
'Tez a boy an' a maid in a country glade,
A story as you've often heard.

How the boy lost his heart to the maid.
Well, the how of it's always the same,
'Tez where I met Nellie that I wants to tell 'ee,
She was rending the butter and craim.

In a Cornish kitchen,
With the log fire glow on the wall,
And the nickety 'nock of the grandfather clock,
The blue and white china and all.

The floor clean and sanded,
The table for supper was laid,
Her mother said "stay", well, what could I say?
So I sat beside Jan's little maid.

Old Jan farmed about forty acres,
And I was his bettermost man,
So 'twas easy for me to be seeing of she,
And that's how the courting began.

On Easter Day, just a year after,
Us off to church prinky dressed,
I gived her the ring and all that sort of thing,
And the parson chap he done the rest.

We've a Cornish kitchen,
There's a squab pie steaming,
The table for two neatly laid
A chair for me, and another for she,
What was Farmer Jan's little maid.

I've seen chaps look as wisht as a winnard,
What you call "scared out of their life"
Perhaps starved as a baby, or poor liver, maybe,
But 'tis most times a troublesome wife.

Of course, all the maids aren't like my maid,
What a joy of a world it would be,
If such maids could be found to have one each all round,

6

And all be as happy as we.

Chorus:
We've a brave fine boiling,
The table for three is laid,
That's Nellie and me, and the other you see,
Is our own little, dear little maid.

MAZED MONDAY

When mining was in full swing in Cornwall the day on which the miners received their pay was known as Mazed Monday in West Cornwall.

The farmhouse at Glebe Farm, Sancreed, was at that period the local inn known as "The Bird in Hand" and some reminders of the pastimes in which the miners indulged are still extant. This was a time for great jollification and a three acre field known as the Plen-an-gwarry was used for sports which consisted chiefly of wrestling and donkey races. Donkeys were used for transport by many of the miners but, in the races no one was allowed to ride his own donkey and the prize was won by the rider of the donkey who finished last.

The adjoining field, known as the Bowling Green, is on a higher level and made an ideal grandstand when sports were in progress below. A small enclosure near the inn was known as Keel Alley, a corruption of Skittle Alley. It is said that when mining declined at Sancreed the unemployed miners were not allowed parish pay unless they carried a sack of sand to the top of the Beacon and brought it back again.

LIME OR WHITEWASH

Lime or whitewash was used extensively in the early days of the century both indoors and outdoors. It was a pretty sight to see our cottages gleaming white in the sunlight after their annual facelift, very often done prior to the parish feast. Dairies in farmhouses were whitewashed annually with a touch-up of lower areas in between and the walls of the "shilter" or cowhouse received similar treatment.

Prior to being used for this purpose the lime had to be quenched with water and this necessitated careful handling as a blob of lime in one's eye could cause severe discomfort, but on one occasion the damage proved to be much more painful. It happened in the parish of Sancreed when a farmer and his son were quenching lime in an old seventeen gallon milk churn. Suddenly there was an explosion and the churn rose about 20 feet in the air and then dropped on the roof of a shed where the farmer had run for shelter and came through causing the occupant a deep cut on his head and bruised shoulders. Luckily his son ran in the opposite direction and escaped injury.

ALL FOR HET AN' PILCHARDS

Another old saying, but alas, "pilchurs" or "pilshies", as we used to call them, seem to be very scarce these days. In the early part of this century pilchards were very plentiful and cheap and were purchased in large numbers for use in the winter months when fresh fish was scarce. They were laid down in salt in a large earthenware pot known as a "bussa" and cooked when required. Pilchards cooked on an open fire were known as scrowlers and one often saw unsalted fish hanging on a stick outside cottage doors after being split open and cleaned.

Hawkers of fish were known as jousters and usually kept a pony and trap for this purpose. One would hear the vendor long before he came in sight shouting 'pilchie' or 'mackurl'. A neighbour's cat sat too close to the wheel one day and later found himself minus a tail. Fishermens' wives walked around the streets selling fish which they carried in a back-basket known as a cowal. It was not unusual to purchase a hundred pilchards for sixpence in the height of the season. According to an old saying it was unlucky to eat pilchards from the head downwards, eating from tail to head brought fish to the shore. Fingers were used to eat them; prongs were for meat.

Many years ago large quantities of pilchards were exported to Italy and the following rhyme relates to this –
Here's to the health of the Pope! May
    he live to repent
and add just six months to the term of
    his Lent,
And tell all his vassals from Rome to
    the Poles,
There's nothing like pilchards for saving
    their souls.

PENNIES OF YESTERYEAR

What a joy it was to have a penny to spend; but what a problem making up one's mind what to purchase from all the "niceys" on display and how patient the shopkeeper was with customers who dilly-dallied before deciding. Large glass jars contained all sorts of brightly coloured sweets, bars of chocolate were a penny or a halfpenny according to size, a packet of sherbet was a penny or one could have a long strip of liqourice with a squeaker on the end. A penny would also purchase a lucky packet and four caramels, but prettily coloured scented cachous were great favourites with girls, whilst a boy might choose the flat round sweets with a sentimental motto, maybe shyly presenting one with the words 'I love you' to a girl he fancied.

GOOK

Probably the word "gook" is now known mainly by older folk, but it is not generally known that most likely it came from the old Cornish word "cugh", meaning a head covering. Commonly known today as sun-bonnets, years ago gooks were "oal tha wor" as the old saying goes. Children wore them to school and women wore them when helping with the corn harvest, but they are mainly associated with the bal maidens sorting out the ore brought up from the mines and various other tasks. Their design varied considerably, as did the materials used. Made chiefly by travelling dressmakers, who carried their own machines to work, some were quite elaborate with tucks and frills, others quite plain, perhaps made from material left over from father's "stripey" shirt!

Traditionally associated with gooks and white aprons, bal maidens could only wear this attire in fine weather. Often working ourdoors in drenching rain they worked long hours and were poorly paid.

"A GWENNAP BAL MAIDEN'S CHAUNT"

The following rhyme recorded by C.C. Thomas in a history of Gwennap refers to the types of work done by bal maidens

I can buddy, and I can rocky,
And I can walk like a man,
I can lobby (toss) and shaky
And plaise the old Jan

LIKE A GANDER GEEKIN' IN A BUSSA

So goes the old saying referring to a curious person (geekin' means peeping) and a bussa was an old earthenware salting pot.
It is quite surprising how many old sayings and superstitions are

connected with birds. 'As tender as a chick', as Billy said when he was eating muggety pie, the latter consisting of sheep's entrails, parsley and cream, but the word muggety was also used to describe an ill-tempered person.

It was said that if a cock crew at midnight the angel of death was passing over and a robin tapping at a window was a warning of trouble, or, if it was heard chirping mournfully, sad news could be expected. If a robin came into a house, it was a sure sign that a fatal illness would attack one of the family shortly. A raven croaking over a house foretold ill to some member of the family. Bird cages used to be draped with crepe when there was a corpse in the house.

"Kill a robin or a wran (wren), never prosper boy nor man," was another saying, and it was unlucky to kill a Cornish chough.

One might still be informed that if there was enough frost before Christmas to hold up a duck, all the rest of the winter would be muck.

Probably there is still superstition extant about magpies. Men used to raise their hats when they saw one to counteract any ill-feeling. Now it gets a salute instead.

Names of birds figure in regional nicknames such as Polruan Polly Roosters, Padstow Crows, Whitstone Owls and Launcells Geese.

FARM PLACE NAMES IN WEST CORNWALL

Composer unknown

Tregonebris, Embla, Brejia,
Menadarva, Trevaneague,
Tregaminion, Foage, Trevega,
Trowan, Trewey, Reskageague.

Carn Kenedjick, Castle, Skewjack,
Tregavara, Trink, Resteague,
Vellanoweth, Bosporthennis,
Wicca, Brunnion, Ventonleague.

Amalwhidden, Carnequidden,
Gear Noon Gumpus, Penderleath
Amalebra, Carn, Chytodden,
Chun, Conswinsawsen, Gear, Rospeath.

FARM PLACE NAMES IN MID-CORNWALL

K. Hawke

Penventinue, Mennabilly,
Trezare, Penant, Treesmill,
Treverran, Polglaze, Pentillie,
Trenant, Colwith and Trill.

Trevenna, Yeate, Trenadlyn,
Polhormon, Carne, Poldew,
Penhale, Lantyne, Lamellyn,
Carneggan, Cornhill and Rew.

Lawhyre, Leyonne, Polscoe,
Penpol, Lankelly, Pelean,
Roselyon, Lampetho, Lescrow,
Coombe, Towan and Colligreen.

HITHER AND THITHER IN CORNWALL

The Treffry Viaduct which spans Luxulyan Valley is 100 feet high and cost £7000 to build.

Temple is the smallest churchtown in Cornwall.

The earliest known book printed in Cornwall is a volume of poems by N. James printed at Truro, 1742.

Mary Bowden, who died in the year 1815, was a member of the religious body known as Quakers. At her request her body was interred under the seat where she sat in the meeting place at Halbethic, near Liskeard.

Mevagissey was the first town in Cornwall to be lit by electric, the year, 1896.

Passmore Edwards, in his biography, tells about a visit he made to Bodmin in 1840 to see the hanging of two brothers called Lightfoot, condemned for the murder of Neville Norway. Edwards walked from Truro, covering a distance of 44 miles there and back.

Nanswhyden, St. Columb Major, built in 1740 at a cost of £30,000, was destroyed by fire in 1803.

Richard Lower, of Tremere, St. Tudy, born in 1631 was the first to perform the operation of blood transfusion.

William O'Bryan, born at Gunwen Farm, Luxulyan in 1778 was the founder of the Bible Christian denomination.

Pencarrow was the first home in Cornwall for the tree Araucaria imbricata, commonly known as Monkey Puzzle. A visitor, having made too close an inspection, remarked, "It would be a puzzle for a monkey."

At a magistrate's court of Petty Sessions held at the Porcupine Inn, Tywardreath Highway, in the year 1842, two persons were charged with being tipsy on a Sunday and were fined 7s 6d or to sit six hours in the stocks.

Launceston Gaol was closed in 1829 on completion of the new County Prison at Bodmin.

In October, 1799, the Cornwall Agricultural Society organised a ploughing match at Wadebridge in which 29 ploughs competed. The ploughs were drawn by oxen.

George William Manning, former rector of Little Petherick, was said to have had his coffin made some years previous to his death in 1876. When completed, he at first slept in it, but latterly on it.

The village of Bugle took its name from an inn around which it grew. The Royal Cornwall Gazette of 1840 states – the miners and clayworkers in the vicinity of Roche Rock have, of late, been duly gratified by the musical performances of Channon. The name Bugle was assigned to the newly erected inn as a compliment to Channon's ability on that instrument.

A Hard Question

"How many do you think oft to zing a zolo?" is the question put to the narrator by a Parish Clerk. The choir were preparing a Christmas anthem, in which there was a solo, and some members thought five men would be needed to sing it, but the clerk thought three would be sufficient to "zing any zolo". He was the leader of the choir, and when asked if he played the organ said, "us ain't got no organ; our folks out there don't hold wi' it". But they were not without music – "We have got a vlute, an' a sarpint and a base vial; and sometimes Kit Thomas cometh and help'th with 'is fiddle." He was made happy by being gravely told that three men would be sufficient to sing a solo.

(Westcountry Dialect Stories)

The Old Wagons

Prior to the coming of the railway to Cornwall in 1852, long distance travel was catered for by Russell's horse-drawn wagons. At a dinner at Helston in August 1846, to celebrate the passing of the West Cornwall Railway Bill, a song was sung:

"Russell's Wagon, 'tis said,
With eight horses well fed,
 Took ten days to creep on the old way
From Falmouth to London.
And then it was scarce done
 For want of a West Cornwall Railway
"Now Russell, 'tis said,
And his horses are dead,
 All quitted the world in the old way.
A better man never lived,
 And better horses not bred,
But they could not keep pace with the Railway"

1852

(Writer unknown – manuscript)

13

On the twenty-fifth of August
The trains are going to run,
From Penzance up to Truro,
And we shall have some fun.

The line is laid both firm and strong,
The carriages are sure,
They're fit to carry England's Queen,
And made to suit the poor.

Chorus:
Then let the bells all ring,
And let the music play,
Come lads and lasses one and all,
To the Railroad haste to away.

Advertising in 1812

An early travelling trader called himself "Earl James". He travelled the
country in great style, with "A large commodious shop drawn by Eight
Greys". On one occasion he printed his price list:

For eighteen-pence a pair of hose,
And Chemise for one shilling;
At James's shop, full stout and good,
For ready money selling.

As winter now approaches fast
And flannels are not dear,
A Petticoat for twenty-seven pence
For Ladies fit to wear.

And to complete this charming dress,
Materials you may buy
To make a Bonnet neat and good
For sixpence-half-penny.

THIS, THAT AN' T'OTHER

Come all you good Cornish boys walk in,
Here's brandy, rum and shrub and gin,
You can't do less than drink success
To copper, fish, and tin.

Cock a doodle do!
Gramma's lost her shoe,
Down by the barley moo,
And what'll Gramma do?
Cock a doodle do!

Ee's pinnikin, palchy, an' totelin', an' ee's clicky an' clappy, an' kiddles an' quaddles all day.

Definition –

He is little, weakly imbecile, he is left-handed and lame, and he fidgets idly about all day.

It is lucky if a stray swarm of bees settles near your house, so throw a handkerchief over it to claim it.

Honey should be taken on St Bartholomew's Day, as he is the patron saint of bees.

To prevent a cold, eat a large apple at Hallowe'en under an apple tree just before midnight. No other garment than a bed sheet should be worn (a kill or cure remedy!)

GIRLS' CHRISTIAN NAMES 1611 - 1705

Redyan	Modesty	Elizabetha
Luzelia	Duance	Margeria
Armonella	Candace	Emblinge
Vesitta	Orpha	Agneta
Sapience	Bathsheba	Immelinam
Hephezibah	Petronellam	Christabellam

15

COUNTING THE FISH

Composer unknown

Waun day 'twas fish in Sennen Cove;
  Aw passel o' men wor theer,
Says Ebby's Jack, "Tes plain to me,
  Tha fish arn't counted feer,
Fifty wor catched and broft ashore,
  I knaw that very well;
There's two wor gove to Peggy's Grace,
  The others we must sell".
"Aw lie! Aw lie!" say Peter's Dick:
  "Aw wadden no shus thing;
There worn't but thirty mellards catched,
  And haaf-aw-dozen ling."

Says Mary's Jack to Peter's Tom,
  "I seed them oal broft in;
'Tea bad enuff to tell aw lie,
  But chaiten' es a sin!"

"An' who's aw bigger chait then thee?"
  Says Matthew's Marget Ann,
"Thees oft to hold tha tung, I'm sure,
  Thee arn't but hafe aw man."
"An' who art thee." says Nancy's Tom,
  "With fringe about the head?
Thee cussen't maake aw pasty yet,
  Nor baake aw batch of bread.
Thee cussen't darn aw stocken, yet,
  Nor make aw heavy caake;
Thee hasn't sense to milk aw cow,
  Nor boil aw bit of haake!
Thee cussen't draw aw tetie, yet,
  Nor mait aw little pig!
Thee cussen't maake aw figger yet,
  Thee cussen' write nor read;
And aw uglier faace than thee hast got,
  I'm sure I never seed!"

"Good loar's aw fuss", says Stevey's Grace,
  "About aw few ole ling!
I wedden make aw row like that
  About aw bigger thing".

"Come on, come on," says Sampey's Joe,
  "And laive us act like men;
Fifty wor catched I'm sure of et!
  We'll count the fish agen."
"My gosh!" says Nancy's Ned to Bill,
  "Es time to go to say;
We've thrawed away aw hour or more
  Le's have aw dish o' tay!"

Moral –
Whenee'r you differ on a point,
  Think on the words you use,
And if you can't see eye to eye,
  Don't bother and abuse

THE LAND OF THE SAINTS

K Hawke

St. Levan, St. Agnes, St. Just, St. Feock
St. Germans, St. Clement, St. Allen, St. Breock
St. Veep, St. Clether, St. Erth, St. Gennys,
St. Columb, St. Blazey, St. Eval, St. Dennis

St. Keverne, St. Minver, St. Ives, St. Mellion.
St. Winnow, St. Tudy, St. Cleer, St. Endellion,
St. Breward, St. Neot, St. Ervan, St. Kew,
St. Pinnock, St. Wenn, St. Merryn, St. Ewe

OLD COB WALL

By: C. Fox Smith

The old cob wall   Us propped en up
Have fell at last;   With stones and 'ood
We knawed he might   Us done our best
A good while past   But 'twerent no good

17

Great-grandad, he
Built thicky wall
With maiden earth
And oaten strawl

He built en in
The good old way
And there he've stood
Until today

But wind and rain
And frost and snow
Have all combined
To lay'en low

He gived a bit
And then a lot,
And at the finish
Down he squat

And now since barns
Has got to be
Us built another
'Stead of he

But not the same's
He was afore
'Cos no one builds
Cob walls no more

SAYINGS USED IN CORNWALL

Going at it like a bull at a gate
'Tez so broad's 'tez long
They wuz having a proper slinging match (dispute)
She'd skin a flea for a farthing
For pity's sake stop gulging, you'll chuck yerself (eating quickly; choke)
She's a proper wild-de-go (rash; reckless)
Dressed up like a lawyer
Looking like a dying duck in a thunderstorm

Like a fly in a jam pot (can't keep still)
Wear pink to make the boys wink
Can't blow nor strike (perplexed)
I forgot myself (went to sleep)
Worse than a flea to catch (never home)
Always on the randy (never home)
It's a sin to steal a pin, let alone a bigger thing
Healthy as a trout
We don't pull and drag Sundays (shake mats)
Like a toad under a harrow (weighed down)
Straight as a pound of candles (good character)
The old must go, the young may go
Flowers fade on flirts
Gulls crying were said to be the souls of men crying to be saved
Aw gate knaw nothing gwain nowheer (stupid person)
Always ill and sickly, more likely to live than die quickly
Hung up his hat (said of a young man invited in to supper by his lady love)
Going like a lamplighter
You'd think money grew upon ferns (said of a spendthrift)
Take yer hands out yer pockets, they'll look like want catchers' pockets (want – mole)
Will 'ee have a drop of warm? (a cup of tea)
Hitched up (said of children not looked after)
Deaf on one ear and can't hear on the other
Going up tembern hill (going to bed)
Looking like a winnard (looking cold)
The poor soul was in some taking (upset)
As drunk as a Piraner
Pride is never cold
As good as a Christmas play
Three on one horse like going to Morvah Fair
Lost your appetite and found a donkey's
Don't know and won't be told
Running round like a scalded cat
Strong in the hand, weak in the head
Bossed about like stinking fish
If there's any difference they're both alike
The Lord will provide, if He doesn't He isn't to His promises

Carn Brea Castle

SAYINGS CONNECTED WITH THE WEATHER

Fools are weather wise,
Those that are weather wise
Are rarely otherwise

Farmers believed that to thrive they should rise with the 'craw',
And go to bed with the 'yaw' (ewe)

A February spring is not worth a pin,
A wet June makes a dry September

Cornwall will stand a shower every day
And two for Sunday

A north wind is a broom for the Channel

A Saturday's moon is a sailor's curse
Friday's moon is Sunday's doom
There's never a Saturday in the year
but what the sun it doth appear

Rooks darting around a rookery, sparrows twittering,
donkeys braying are signs of rain

Cats running wildly about the house
said to bring storms in their tails

Before the end there will be no difference between summer and winter
save in the length of the days and the green of the leaf (erroneously said
to be mentioned in the Bible)

NAMES FOR TOOLS AND OTHER ARTICLES

Axe (large) – mod axe
Boring tool (long) used my miners – gad
Brake on wagon wheel – drug
Bucket with rope for well water – draw bucket
Bucket for use in mine – kibble
Body of cart – butt
Cask or tub (large) – tonnel, tunnel
Cask (small) used by smugglers – anker
Cobbler's anvil mounted on wooden leg – bickern
Coconut fibre broom – caihar broom
Digger (two clawed) for digging turf – tubbal

21

Dish or pan – paddick, parrick, pattick (or could be an earthenware pitcher)
Double headed tool for digging – biddix
  ditto (with long ends) – visgy
Drill – boryer
Drill (pointed) used in a mine – moil
Earthernware salting pot – bussa, stain, stein, stug
Earthernware crock – pan crock
Farm implement used to pound and cut beards from barley in winnowing – piler
Flail thresher – drasher, drasser
Flat iron – stile
Fork – prong, evil, heaval
Gophering iron – jinny quick
Hammer (small) used for breaking up tin – cobbing hammer
Hamper – mawn, maund
Hogshead – osgit
Hook for putting corn in sheaves – rulling hook
Hook with slight curve – patch hook
Keg – cag
Mason's drill – point
Miller's wooden measure – pottle
Milk pan – panshon
Miner's small axe – dag
Part of plough – gruter
Pot or baker under which bread was baked in burning wood ashes – wilver
Prop or underset to a lever – colpas
Rasp – raps
Shovel – showl
Slate axe – shaddocks
Sledge for carrying stones – draw, drag
Small solid wheel – druckshar
Spear (3 pronged) for catching fish – grail
Spring balance – stilliers
Spukes – pig's rings
Stone jar (quart size) – Stacey jar
Thatching sticks – brooches, spooks
Tool for ramming down blasting material – tamlyn timbal, tamping iron
Toasting rack – griddle
Tub – keeve
Water keg – breaker

Weeding tool (long handle and thin blade) – paddle
Whetstone – barker
Wooden barrel fixed on wheelbarrow for carrying water – anker and
    dandy,

POLPERRO

NAMES FOR BIRDS

Bittern – clabiter, clobiter
Blackbird (female) and thrush – greybird
Blue titmouse – allecompanie, elecompanie, eckemoule, hekymal,
    pednpaley, prid prad, priden prall
Bullfinch – budpicker, hoop
Buzzard – kit
Chaffinch – apple bird, chiff chaff, copper finch, tink
Cockerel – stag
Chough – chaw, rid-legged chaulk
Cormorant or sea raven – trainy-goat
Crossbill – chipper, shell apple
Curlew – curly
Fighting – chanticleer
Green woodpecker – woodwall
Grey gull – wagel
Guillem (sea bird) kiddaw
Guillemot – mor, mur ·

Guinea fowl – gleany
Hawke (species of) hobbies, lannard, marlion
Heron – crane
Jack snipe – Dame ku, hatter flitter
Jay – janner
Kestrel – cliff hawke, creshock
Landrail – corncrake
Lapwing – cornwhilen
Magpie – johnner, maggety pie
Missel thrush – holm scritch, home scritch
Partridge – rudge
Pigeon (young) – squab
Plover, Peewit, Lapwing – horneywink
Puffin – pope
Redwing – jennard, chywollack, winnard, swellack
Redstart – fire tail
Ring-tailed Kite – fuz kite
Robin – rabin, rudbreast, ruddock
Starling – stare
Shell drake – buranet
Snipe – snite
Stone chat – fuzz chet
Stormy petrels – Mother Carey's chickens
Thrush – throstel
Tom-tit – see blue titmouse
Turkey – lubbercock, lubberleat
Wagtail – tinner, dishwasher
Water hen – fencock, vencock
Water rail – fencock, vencock
Wheatear – chicker, chickchafer, nacker
Wimbrel – May bird
Wren – wranny

NAMES FOR FLOWERS

Arum lily – devil's candle
Antirrhinum – calves' snout
Broom – bannel
Burdock – butterdock, cocklebells, cockle buttons, cuckledock, sticky
    buttons
Camomile – camels

24

Charlock – charlick

Columbine – stocking and shoe, boots and shoes, granny's bonnet or nightcap

Common sorrel – green sauce, sour sauce, sour sabs, sour saps, sour dock

Cow parsley, hogweed, – cowflap, cowflop, keggies, lizzams

Convolvulus – bind weed, drayler, drill drolls

Cuckoo pint – Lords and ladies, preacher in his pulpit

Deadly nightshade (berries) – dogs chuckers

Fennel – love entangle

Feverfew, Featherbow – bothem

Foxglove – pop-dock, poppydock popglove

Fushsia – dropper

Elder – scawsy buds, (blossom) ilder blowth

Germander speedwell – bird's eye

Goosegrass – bilder, cleaver, cliver

Gorse – furze, fuzz

Greater stitchwort – cats' eyes

Ground ivy – halehoof

Heath or Ling – bazaam, griglans, grylans, (dried stalks used for brooms)

House leek – ollick

Hydrangea – Botany Bay, high angels

Ivy leaf toad flax – Mother of thousands

Laburnum – golden chain

Lady's smock – milkmaid

Lungwort – William and Mary

Marsh iris – flag, lidden

Marsh marigold – king cup

Meadow sweet – queen of the meadows

Mountain ash – care

Mouse-ear hawk weed – felon herb

Nightshade – scaw coo

Ox-eye daisy – gadavraws

Pansy – heartease

Periwinkle – gweens, queens, wrinkle

Pennywort – penny-cakes, pancakes

Pink campion – cock robin

Plantain – hard heads, cocks and hens

Scabious (blue) – devil's button, devil's bit

Scarlet pimpernel – poor man's weather glass

Sea anemone – bloodsucker
Sea aster – starwort
Sea dock – bloddy sea dock
Sea nettle – blubber, sting blobbers
Sea weed – flote oar
Self heal – sicklewort
Shepherd's purse – pickpocket
Soleil d'or – butter and eggs
Southernwood – boys' love, maidens' delight
Stingless nettle – blind nettle
Stitchwort – adders' spit
Stock – gillyflower, jellyflower
Valerian – blouncing Bess
Verbena – lemon plant
Wallflower – bloody warrior
Whitethorn (hawthorn) – May blossom
White clover – quillet
Wild hemp – deaf nettle
Wild saffron (Ephiphany custus epithymum) grows over gorse, reddish
   hue
Willow catkins – lambs tails, cats and dogs, goslings, pussy willows

FISH NAMES

Allis shad – alley, chuck cheeld
Angle fish – round robin
Bream (young) – crabalogin
Cray fish – gaver
Cuttle fish – cuddle, coodle, goil
Cuttle fish (big) – pedalinken
Dog fish – dogga, morgy, murgy
Dog fish (lesser, spotted) – culver hound
Eel – eyle
Eel (fresh water) – valsen
Garfish – horn fish
Gurnard – ellick, illick
Haddock – haddick, huddock
Hake – tin sack
Halibut – Jew's fish
Horse mackerel – scad, shad
Lamprey – lamper
Mackerel – brale, breel, brithel
Minnow – mimsie
Monk fish – angel main, mulvannah
Newfoundland cod – niflin, toe rag
Pilchard – pilchie, pilchur
Pilchard (cured) – fairmaid, furmade
Red herring – sodger
Red gurnard – tub
Sea pike – long nose
Sea trout or bull trout – truff
Sprat – herring bairn
Star fish – clam
Stickleback – bulgrannick
Whistler fish – gerrick
Whiting (salted and dried) – buckhorn
Whiting pollack – pouting
Wrasse – Jacky Ralph, guckoo, row

Kynance Cove.

2571. CORNER OF NEWLYN HARBOUR, PENZANCE.

Lamorna Cove.

28

NAMES FOR TREES, FRUITS AND NUTS

Acorn – oakmass, oakmuck
Apple (stunted) – squinge grub
Apple (bright red) – quarantine
Beard of barley – Aile, ile
Brazil nut – pasty nut
Broad beans – mait banes
Bulrush or reed – goss
Cherries (black) – mazzards
Clover – three-leaved grass
Dried Fig – broad fig, dote fig
Damson – bullace, bullums
Dog wood – skiver wood
Earth nut (or pig nut) – fare nuts, killimore, kelly
Elder – scaw, skew, scow or scawen tree
Fir cones – delseed, dealsey
Gooseberry – day berry
Grass (type of) – eavers
Elm – ellum
Haws – aglets, eglets, hoggans, oglans
Hazel bush – nuthall
Hazel nut – cob nut, hall nut, victor nut
Holly – holm, pricklyum
House leek – ollick
Medlars – open asses
Mushroom – pisky stool
Oats – pellas, pillas, pelcorn, wuts
Onions – scullions
Parsley – pane
Pear – peer
Poplars – popples
Potato – poltate, tatie, teddy, tetty
Privet – skedgwith, skerris
Raisin – fig
Shallot (type of) – scifers
Sloes – slones, bullums
Sycamore shoots – May
Turnip – neap, rutabaga, turmot
Whortleberries – urts, whurts

NAMES FOR ANIMALS AND INSECTS

Ant – muryan, emmet
Bat – airymouse, flittermouse
Beach worm – lug
Bee – dumble drain, also given to cockchafer
Bees (swarming) – hez, gliz
Blackbeetle – black worm, snortleywiggan
Blackbeetle (small) for catching trout – fernicock, ferniweb
Blind worm, slow worm – slow cripple
Blue bottle – Mother Margot
Boar – barro, borro
Brown cockchafer – spinning drone
Cat (male) – ram cat
Caterpillar – nanny viper, snortleywink
Cockchafer – May bee, oakweb
Cockerel – stag
Cow (with spotted hide) – vinny cow
Crane fly or Daddy-long-legs – Tommy tailor
Donkey – Jerusalem pony, moke, mawgust, neddy, neggur
Donkeys – kings
Dragon fly – horse adder, noss adder
Drake – mollard
Earthworm – angle dutch, angle twitch, angle touch, tagworm
Ewe – yaw, yow
Ferret – fitcher, fitchett
Fieldmouse – screw
Frog – Quilky, quilkin, culkin, wilky, wilkin
Frog (young) or tadpole – Tom toddy
Gad fly – grey fly, swop, swap
Goat moth – magiowler
Greyhound – long dog
Hare – scavernick, scavarnog, wat, watty
Hedgehog – hedge-a-boar, fuzzy pig
Hen (young) – mabyer
Hybrid between stallion and female ass – moyle
Kitten – chet
Ladybird – God's cow
Lamb (young) – tibby lamb
Lamb (under ten months) – hog lamb
Lice – slow six-legged walkers
Lizard – long cripple

30

Lizard or newt – four legged emmet
Land lizard – sharaligge
Millipede insect – earwig
Mole – moldwarp, want, wont
Mouse – mur (plural) murs
Newt – ebbet, evvet
Newt, eft or lizard – padgy-paw, padgety-paw, padzer-pou
Pig (smallest in litter) – piggywidden, nestlebird, widgan
Pig (young) – slip, veer, vair, sucker
Plymouth Rock pullet – spickety mabyer
Seal – groyne, soyle
Slug – dew snail
Snail – bulhorn, buljink, Jan Jakes, Jan Jeak, Jean Jakes
Snail (small) – sneg
Speckled moth – sound sleeper
Spittle fly – buck
Stoat – fairy weasel, stat
Toad – horneywink
Wasp – apple drane, apple bee, wopse, waps
White throated weasel – whitnick
Woodlouse – grammersow, sow pig, old sow
Worms (small flat worms found in sheep's liver, cause of foot-rot) – iles

Cornwall –" The Village Smithy."

MINING TERMS

Adventure – a working mine
Adventurers – owners of a mine
Attle; Attal – waste earth or stone
Audit; Odit – adit
Balscat, Scat bal – abandoned mine
Balshag – coarse flannel with long nap, used in mines
Bargain – contract for work in a mine
Blawing house – a water blast furnace for tin smelting
Bottoms – old stream works
Bounders – holders of tin bounds
Brace – mouth of shaft
Broil – earth on the surface indicating a vein of metal
Bucking – house for hammering ore
Bucking iron – flat hammer for crushing ore
Buddles – wash tubs for fine ore
Bunching – lode irregularly distributed
Chegwidden Day – one clear week before Christmas when black tin
    was turned into white tin. The day on which white tin (smelted tin) was
    first sold in Cornwall
Cobber – bruiser of tin
Cobbing hammer – small hammer used for breaking tin
Collar boards; Collaring – top board of mine shaft
Cow – windlass with cowl shaped top to supply air in a mine
Dag – miner's small axe
Dowser – forked twig used by miners for divining
Dredgy ore – inferior ore
Elvan – hard rock; porphyries
Fingers – depth of a hole for blasting rock measured by a miner placing
    his fingers against the borer in the hole
Gad – long tool used in mining for boring
Grass – surface mining
Hardah – elvan rock
Huel; wheal – a mine
Hutchwork – small ore worked by a sieve
Jew's house – ancient smelting place for tin
Jew's pieces – ancient blocks of tin
Jigging – process in dressing ore
Kibble, Kibbal – bucket used in a mine
Knacker; Knocker – spirit or little folk in a mine. They were said to be
    the souls of Jews who crippled Christ, sent by the Romans as slaves
    in the mine.

Learys – old mine workings
Lodes – mineral veins
Moil – pointed drill used in a mine
Morion – crystals; Cornish diamonds
Muller – a stone used for reducing tin ore to powder
Mundic – iron pyrites; marcasite
Nickers; Niggies – see knackers
Pair – (of men) a company of men working together on the same bargain
Pair of moyles – usually about fifty mules for carrying tin
Peach – chorite; blueish green soft stone
Piran Day – March 5th; Tinner's holy day.
Pitch – area in a mine to be worked
Prill – mixing rich ore with poor ore to cheat buyer
Ruz – grains of gold, so called by tinners
Scollucks – refuse of slate quarry
Score – tin stuff so rich and pure that it needs little cleaning
Seam of tin – horse load; two small sacks of tin
Shammel whim – engine for drawing ore up over an inclined place
Soller; Saller – stage of boards in a mine
Spaliard – working tinner; a pick man
Spalling – breaking large stones of ore
Spal hammer – hammer used for "spalling"
Spar – quartz
Tamlyn – a miner's tool
Tamping – material used in blasting
Tamping iron – tool for ramming down blasting materials
Timbal – mining tool
Tribute – the share; a share by contract of ore raised, claimed by the
    miner
Troil – a tinner's feast
Trunking – turning up metalliferous slime with a shovel
Tutmen – men who work in a mine by the piece such as sinking shafts.
    driving adits, etc., at so much per fathom
Vanning – trying a sample of ore by weighing it on a shovel
Vugg; Voog – a natural cavity in a mine often found beautifully crusted
    with minerals

Post Office, Buryas Bridge, Cornwall.